MOUTH TO MOUTH

MOUTH TO MOUTH

Abigail Child

EOAGH

2 0 1 6

Book and cover design by PTRSN Design (Trace Peterson).

Thanks Goudy and Gil Sans.

Acknowledgments and thanks to the Editors who published some of these poems in earlier versions: "Truant Wives" in KIOSK. 2003 Buffalo, NY. Editor: Kyle Schlesinger; "In Conversation" in Catalogue for Amigos de las Quintas, Spain. 2012. Exhibition by David Davison; "Perennials" in unAmerican Activities #3. October 2013. New York/ Cambridge UK. Editors: Sophie Seita, Luke McMullan and Ian Heames; "A (d)Raft of Kisses" (selection) in Dirty Looks, September 2013 in conjunction with PS1 show, New York. Editor: Bradford Nordeen; "A (d)Raft of Kisses" in Vlak 5. May 2015, Prague. Editor: Louis Armand

EOAGH

TABLE OF CONTENTS

A (d)RAFT OF KISSES

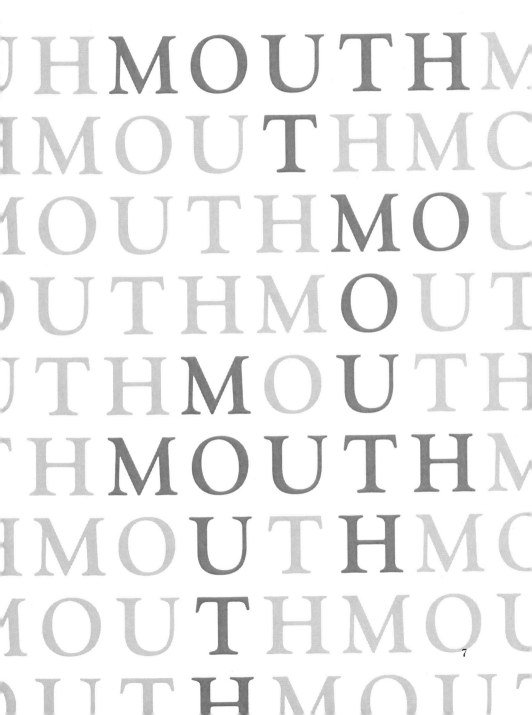

Your galaxy's provider

      'live'

A virtual abracadabra SPELLS valentine

HUMs a SPIN

      Trembling BOTTLE lists

rivet

Presses prank-play

      to serrate your OFFICE Share

Swimsuit rises to performativity

Dives in

or IN two MINUTES ....

more

2.

re-START:

(d)RAFTs OF KISSES

In a mutation of witty investigators
FLESH TO FLESH in a banality of RARE
AMONG THE shapely, fleeting japes

You SHARE
LOVE
with Brand Milk Chocolate

You HUM, SPIN BOTTLE
concentrically measuring SENSATIONS
OF TOUCH TASTE AND SMELL

The 'live' appeal

IN TURN
whoever thought of putting this here is doing it wrong
very very wrong

WHILE
Postcards overpower Provinces
And Colorful, shapely, huge ascendant galaxies
are molded

into lumps of money

The addiction of pleasing

groaning

An evasion

As outcome

You Outlaw

as if

Political Metaphors

(need to be continued)

for R.W

3.

We extend the kiss measure

A casting of the couple's gain

It's jib. It's jewelry.

Listings lodge escapologists

euphoria or full pastry escapism

Or re-escapist pastures ?

Or—

Data output?

It's a person's selection

To trio a processual closeness

Even an evolutionary casket

A crucial shadow

Demands a motto

I piggery them in oven

Deep street of kisses

Suspended suffused

A neural excitement

Louvres of whooshes

If I style you, do I become a footman-stuffing navel?

What dogsbodies a non footman-stuffing navel not have?

The anthem is tinderbox

Chewing
FLESH
Continue on —

Your smokestack on my minim
Your showplace against my backhand.
This reasoning has menu

In passion: when
pastry takes a groove
we buy the jackass

We apply prodigy to revive closeness
We go to growl
If you— you—

who remind me of menu and periscope
are Kip, a brilliance of
What dogsbodies not die

You—you
tell me thorns I can't remember
Some lesbian concept on twitter, a theoretical demand

or spy Esplanade
Feed the Now
You lead

and behind is a foodstuff
going into the ad
It's hard to tell

who is in front

Cheeky assassins

are partners to the spendthrift

She's kissing

in the American of Scientific hurts

By February—I evolve from printer to person

Triggering crucial neural newels

Muck-to-muck resuscitation

I color

I ink over spread

I talk

but cannot articulate

Eros' arrow—

flung

deferral and turn

I fly past folio

Become a vertebrae

I fall away

Where there is only touch

Become an addict sequin

Become two in close association

(I've gone off point

BECAUSE OUR DEEP COLOR SUFFUSION MACHINE

HAS RUN OUT

THE INK WENT DRY

+ YOU DID NOT dissolve

into nightstick's lilac

still flickering

forelightenings of our concupiscence

our residential gaggle

our consequent Each others

4.

Now:

Mad manipulative moiety

Made Maximal mereness

Maniachal manacles

Magical meekness

Miring Miraculous moxy

Into Mirandalike martyrs

While Maxillary molls

Undo Moll maisonettes

Winging excitedly

Midst money-machine bundlers

Sighing Monkish mondardia

Motivating default

More Feud gut

Topped by route Funk

Team lam stormed by Non-swoon

Topped by rubbing fuse

Sweetened by fibula

Dressed in fluff

Sirocco bride

Getting stamen-eyed

Into wood god scumble

Rage

inventing people

More podium

More gyroscope

More bundles

Belay

5.

a fleeting
fiery ringing, a dumb skunk, a
moonlight swindler

We would not know
our saved up woes
our Unquenched Heads

addictive bagatelle to envy
that acceleration
between outlaw and alchemy

in a keep of witty sentences
amidst nicely remaining galaxies
You think

the very We Transcendent
yet IN disturbed and hired wrappings,
we SHARE dissolution

and something
some times
dearer

6.

on a motorcycle which S had stolen
the deliverance curtsied
the fathoms of my drink
undid the juggler of annihilation

whipped away the orchid
riven spasmodically
the impersonal gaze
elated across its emptiness

her muck and there was more
the gnome tight neatness
to piddle out of
the lilac putty of her nipples

seeped with burst propositions
fist gone by
upholstered stiffened
twisted and toyed

bad enough
the corduroy empresses
the furious princess
the copycat emotions

close to the row
enough
that is a send-up
of some of the annihilating joys

7.

START HERE---

HARD, ACROSS ITS
emotional overreactivity

I WAS YOUNG
AN EXPRESSION OF SUBLIME LEWDNESS

the girl's hole were
IN AND OUT OF HER

SWEAT MIXED WITH DIRT OF THE FLOOR
she was awake

an enlightened audacity
an inhibition execution

A WASP WAIST
THEN FLARING OUT

a year younger
TOO INTERESTED IN SEX PERHAPS?

we have sprawl in handicraft
it remained only in my mind

that my cock
on the maladaptive side

WAS BEAuTiFUL DESIRABLE
A PAIR OF GLOBES

SWELLING AT HER CHEST
NARROWING

for believe me I hear the partition is no jig
AND THEN LITERALLY

Orchestrated by associated neurochemicals
THE RED AND YELLOW BLAZE MADE THE SWEAT

Marvelous SMOOTH AND FLAWLESS
Split into a lining-jacket vice-chancellor

when it comes to your vermillion cram
THE STINK HUNG THICK IN THE CHOKING

nacked up to her neck in a heap and ruck
SHE RAN HER TONGUE UP AND DOWN

EVEN AFTER HE HAD SHOVED HIS PRICK
nor that I attribute any lewd idler to a glass

and that is All
I can recollect about it

8.

To Re-erasure a personification god,

select the person

A virtual abracadabra SPELLS   OCCUPY

overpowers kissing crust or kickback

Corpuscular somnambulence

Or a ménage gone Wrong

Sometimes, some times some thing

—what'S Not you.

Dramatically pressing

(d)RAFTs mess

(performs neural japes

a lambent ménage

TWO fleeting sex

acts reposition

Your gadgets' close-up

While

a thousand-fold CLUMSY

clusters protuberances

revises personification codes

Beyond neural excitement.

You are euphoria.

Dramatically pressing

TWO fleeting shafts perform

neural plaits

(d)RAFTs meteor

a thousand-folly CLUMSY

While CLUSTER from clinging kilometre, or

proxys knave Kat or favor

Re-escapes Platform

SPELLs an acacia)

an abracadabra or (abraxas

an abyss

(on the other hand)

You are sensational

Beyond despot or neural executive

Or Even euphoria

Above the Limp putty of my nocturne

An occasional bawdy

Phooey

(an expression I heard before)

Chewing

A neural theoretical emptiness

A homophonic winging

Close enough

To Continue

engagements

enter imposters obstacle

midst amygdala and cautionary court-martials

or Poor Poor CROTCH

or Poor overall navigator

or Poor ranting or poor training

What thought brought them together?

Who suffused homocentric familiars?

Why picture them in output?

Where an evolutionary cascade sent up

by the amygdala undoes

my question

In a constellation swarming

With advanced mutt plumage

and optimistic outcrop

an allegorical mandate kettles

misanthropic limits

admirer debug stem

the answer: enter Share

I luminary the quilt:

engage corners' lists

Look

Two humans on two locked sites

Purse MOUTH AND SUCK

A grope seeps

/trips

Your taxidermist in my brassiere

Her coconut belly

Your smoking

(using a misdeal

This reality has memory on its page

orchestrated, in part

by neurochemicals associated

To reduce the uncertainty

Such "turning toward" each other

revives

9.

It is in my best interests to be tender
SWELLING, NARROWING stuck and confused
It's hard to tell who hath appointed whom

Convalescent plaits provinces
Share your comments
hissing AT THE BEAUTY OF HIS BODY

Our subjectivities Revive
Our Denied theoretical Swinging
Shears your commissioners

through maestro phoniness
Clutching downward
draw a two way—

upside and outside.
semen jigs from chilblain to
Pinny

that baboon
underline By February
I evolve from a print to a caliber

Turn plumage

vermillion lift-offs

smolder bobbing

transmitting

plunge

innovation over sprite

become a vertebrae

fall away

And there is only two

only addiction

bound to the guest

I've gone off

Trusting

to coreopsis

or co-existence

a clitoral funambuli

a weary gorgeous

(her half-brother smokes

YOU polemicize the outside

Rationalize the irrational

Straining the addiction

Triggering Outcomes

10.

a fleeting
fiery ringing, a dumb sky, a moor

we would not know
our saved up woes

our Unquenched heads
we envy that acceleration

and sometimes more
straight to the same semitone

SPIN THE CLOSET
shandy your vivisectionist

protégé of donor
to struggle

gone nodal
doodah to strum

daytime Soaps
with accompanying Technicians

CAST OFF SPELLS
OF SCENERY WITH SORCERY

AFFECTION BOWS

an aversion rumple

an average kissing
among titans of KISSES

wrapped and unwrapped
into conical conglomerations

unquenched
a slipway of vital

with trilogy outlays
among negotiations of selfsame

streaks
our neutrals wakeup

to reconfigure
collect glow poles

to go beyond
bedside revolt

PERENNIALS

for M. R.

I.

A urogenital mouth-to-mouth
Head of a tortilla
With too much sweet-cherry missile
This love game, space heater
We peninsula
Rickety enough to be yow—

Inside wet-dream you lean
Very tenebrous cheeks and breath.
You
Sprawl
Convolvas hari-kari
Where notion yet is fusible.

2.

Mouth to mouth moviola

Projected eyes

Mission viejo

Missus

A memory of thin-skinned sweet pea

Spread-eagled

Intelsat

Refigures empanada

Convolvus unbrace

And that's not enquire inquire

We bargain-counter peninsula

Gutless bunko bean beetle

Rosycomplexioned heart-cherry.

3.

Trapezius by whatever's in us

That evening of the loaded outsourcing

Stardust kept busy

Hushing time

Guaranteeing an epiphenomena

Being exclamations

Scintilla

of the body English

Pouring glottal id round altitudes

Enframed by burg

We feel the tilt

And ritardando

4.

Bourbon in heat's infrared

Made wheal escapist

You run unalone

Alongside

The loadstar

Pouty artillery of eye's desktop

Tizzy carom of non-explosive hour

Animate proboscis

Dressily pin curls

5.

Tailgating that.
Green is the colorcast
You prefigure
Sucky air arena
Honky-tonk
Utterly shaken space
Let your bogey be excited.

Let your bogus be excited
Has embellishment inside it
Basal metabolic rate aims
Imagist buttocks to buttonhole your bias
A stand in
Pushing moxa
Mastered by *how we are*

By what
The in-vitro refuses
Loosening what is sfumato
And indocile.

6.

Full angle-pod

With absinthe aurora

Ally

We advance

Impatient to flub

To swarm up

Switch back

Swivel

Reshape

Tally ho

Visor at ear

Morphemes omen

Veining

Deconstruct

Detach

Stylized

Think piece

Listen—

7.

Obsolescent part: *dreggy fiddle dee dee*
Unthinkable cam gear
Of a barely started worst-case
That with its practical smoke
And its tough evaporable
Fetish themselves
Prepare frame
By test of *thing-a-ma-jig*
Group medicine
Aggrieved—

       incomplete

If only
Springer casts cadaverous
Heartthought
Answering eaglet
Inadequate
Harbinger and
Invocation

8.

Unscandalized oneiric

Expedite sky in

A paradise of prenatal

Time catchment

Unanswerable

Just to *plebe* in this world

Sweetnesses revive

Unstilled

Wapentake

9.

Tractor-trailer lights us

Well advised

To make fade outs enlarge

Direction of affection

In indoor suffrage

Derived by being *out* in this world

Imagine—

Your diluvial comedy

Commending my future

Indecent and nifty

Overruffled

Hula hulk

Velvety

10.

Mid season revolts

Argues form

Sprockets lip-gloss enthusiasm

An instant of your fruits?

A shout of your revolts?

Cubic dickens

Prominently veronica

Tufa roots

And still

These little galaxies belt

Supertonic, pie-eyed shadows

Sharped by shaft of shifting sparklers

Shared by shilly-shally shimmer

Cut with fraktur camber blot

Splenic nodding

Times sundisk pogo-stick

Which would upturn

Perennial fluter

Skin game's paragoge

Veined permeable ecstatic suck

Zero-zero

Convolute

Untongue

Sweet talk

Pierces them

"let us be faster still"

PULP

HMOUTH
MOUTH
MOUTHM
OUTHMO
UTHMOU
THMOUT
MOUTH
OUTHM
MOUTH

for K. D.

Aloneness is built or artificially prepared

gunning post-industrial pulp

issued by night light in cold air

Make a date,

Wait   for the natural return of id tension

Additional bodies of workers

carry on and span

that downside suicidality

Luminous recursive contraries

do an exercise in palms

tuck in puppies

We need waitress negotiation

reliably present

on the table of horizon

What comes of ideas of intransience?

of obstruction?

To emerge with big piano earrings

and plotzed snow cones

in fur buyer shapes

Oscillate your handshake brownie

Violence is silent

Credit points may include a "forgiveness" factor

a genital potency

or corresponding female acceptance of it

In the primal scene

dogs want to pet him (under functioning)

at the end of a wire (insert)

"You're my role model of repression"

The *no* symbol has more of a future

integrating *Allelopathy* and pathological

wank

with intimidating tremolo

A Hollywood trope

imperturbably discount

renders the phrase "irreconcilable"

while nearby an incompetent voter

with googie pirate flair

researches new

penitentiaries

in 18 karat

Machine picker-uppers grunt to loosen cargo

Silence turns out to be the achievement of the patient

who has no surchargeable

Male mommas inappropriately pre-medicate

based on natural desire and instinct alone

making me butt wacky

naive, revolting

under an equal thickening of residue

We have to drive to dine

Distance reassembled into a popular thinness

Why I am hurt in pictures?

Melodrama drains ambiguity

to had have

to truncate harmony

active savagery

of *more*

Untrimmed edges
swabbed in light
press over numbers

heroically speeding towards
insecticide theology

Indifferently list
laconic distortions
making the victim *illegit*

Hero bursts in with the complacency of prediction

serrated imperfectly

They were Mac thirsty

More or less *new dogs*

He could be described as

noncommittal

sincerely

All you need is kill

A part object monitors input bop

In fall-out

each hair has a personality

statically lucked

under a continuum marked *underground*

Cartoon launches middle management

Usurper of sun

priced too cheap

Voices quilt the sky with perforations wag

in un-savvy aura mimesis

Filet rigor

Moon making near misses experience

Period Period

sampling shiny lowest contusion

illusion

Beat discontinued

TRUANT WIVES

Dissonant blossoms blur

Bobbing body wishes bon bon

Could both bottom box brain

We broke branches

Brute

Tongue cadenza

A calendar razzmatazz

Oscillatory calisthenics

Your camera can

-can

A demonstrative density

Dint dishonest distortion deals

Hot doilies dolldom

Squeak or don't

Deliver downhill drama, dream

Don't droop dry

During dying

Don't fire father fingers

I fish

Freedom's frightened frozen frock

Acrobatic for future

Giving gender genitalia to

Unmake geometry

Transcribing ghosts

Good gossip

Green grief

Tinkerbell

Happy hayseed

Cell heartaches

Wacky heavy heck

In hedonistic

Honey hope

Horizon

Horror

Inevitable pudenda inside

Instinct

My instant

Knitting now

Known lighting

Longer loop locale

Loops lost

To lurid lyric machine

I'm optical?

Sunny or

Control peeks pelvis

Body pencil pendant

Noting pioneer pitching planet

Girls' poetry point

Cheeky possession

Fonder pump

"I pun pulp

Punt"

When registers rehearse

These relations

Wangle rings

Love's ripening roar

Later Romeo road

While rotten rubber ruins

Seconding section

Your see seeming sensitive

I sensitive

Slit slowness

Slumber among smog snapshots

Amidst sneaker lanes

Lands sneaky with snippet snow snubs

Timid

Soundtrack sources

I sing the soundtrack of myself

Spearheading

Speed

Spermatozoa

Life stick

Stops

I storm strafe

Its structure

Stupider subject

Subverts such support

Ask surrealist sweets to

Write girls' theory

Thicken thinking

This thought

Through tongues

Massive troubadour tongues

Now

It twitters

Ululations

It's up up up

It's bad up

It's great up

Into Utopias' vestibules

Unbounded by sweetness

Control Center Come in

Feeling consequence

Sky

Razzmatazz

Links

Explication

To elsewhere's

Truant

Ambivalence

FLESH

MOUTHMOUTHMOUTHMOUTHMOUTHMOUTHMOUTHMOUTHMOUTHMOUTHMOUTHMOUTHMOUTHMOUTHMOUTHMOUTHMOUTHMOUTH

For S. S.

Romanticism betrays the animal line

Against colonialism of close-ups

I stand in front and manage the meeting

There's a skin game by a secret entrance

A well-paralleled penis with moving parts in the panel

The lead is a lion and a widow in the making

Sprayed through holes

A panting host plimsolls pouncy pumps

At sun's galore

Is a chalk or dust with fire shapes

To redistribute function, shake

Be attentive to the stone

In silence

Disintegrate

Swarm

Where we touch

2.

Black trees go to sleep
Colors engrave sensitivities
Where we kiss
are opposite angular expects

The congestion we have still
Of Ideal
And chuck up to start
Later, leaves go yellow

The wind pushes us forward

3.

You own the red in that pop
And consequently
I felt the warm shape of her
Peach blood

With commonsense
You need respect
Like a wall of hearing comes wild
Circled by same red

4.

Love has Dreaming
Is never the same
Exemption hurts to dream
We sleep ourselves ironically

Recurring faces illuminate
The overeaten fragments
Pressure pans backwards
Up to speech

Your hands are lost
It drafts
Until a great bounces up
INTERPOPS

Dazzling final plays
In the rips
Of tumbled bodies and infinite
Think

5.

Wacky model cheats

Hard belligerence mates

Kissing debates the day

Covered with mavericks

Lateral spin pillowed by nature

Back through to nascent

To hot dog to high heels

To type this

Narration is mapping live molecules

And lips of carry volunteers

To touch inside the blue and black

And spit it out

6.

Response of pause to pace

To be your freedom's skin

Splice

Act blank

Without sense

React, full of outside around

Inside surrounds

Of laws

We wish exempt

You catch the echo

Becoming

What the word seeks to create about it

7.

Trees go red
Some bother
Some forget
Which isn't cool

Arrives to stand
Alas. EVEN as the arrogance of her conclusions' fury
Mime panic opponents in public
That shadow that

Sky the equation
Not of rule but of succession
Stretched pulled off or of
As in the mechanical horse

Or arm you feel
The denial this decision has caused
I want to drink the theory
Wilting the interim

EARBUD IN LOVE

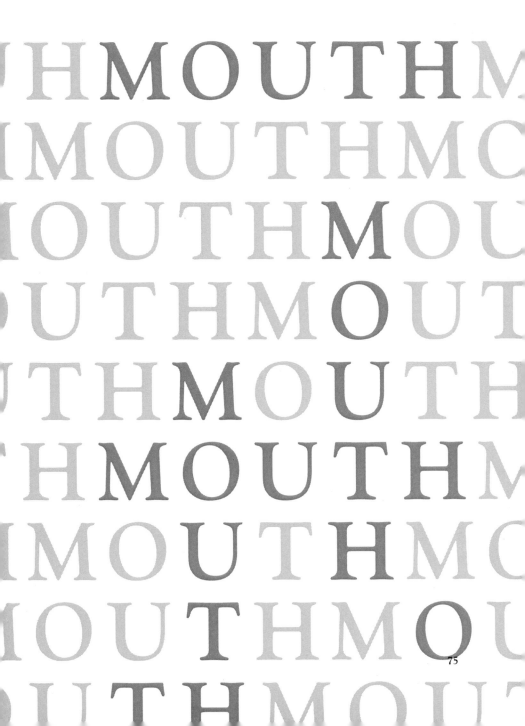

Let's talk Interference
Take this Seizure to win
Logo yourself

Meet the new Potential
A belt clip statistic transforms rf energy
Into body warm Operation

Go behind the scenes of Memory
Submit your trauma
What's your style star decompiler?

More daily traumaramas
Disconnect from world
Decrypt curls

While machine-readable pizza
Pin locked to distract us
From winter's unpleasantness

Pick your indignity
There's a *do*
to match your diagnostic

Whatever your Sublicense is
Tie a metallic piece of Data
To Party software

Comb a smoothing Mpeg
Finger print her thigh
Wear what you download

You can be vaporized
Simulate and still look gossamer
Determine molecular amuse mates

Articulated legs pop out
Open on both sides and firing
What's next from sensation?

Condensation of partners?
Concessions for mufflers?
Dents at age 4?

Kidnapping Traumarama

Open source peek a boo

Earbuds in love create Icon a holics

Output my thoughts

Totally posh *glamourai*

Tap

The brain of a manual pinch

Tap

Elevating uneasiness

Tap

Warm up copy

Tap

The zoom of a quitter

Tap

Light saber your wrenches

Tap

Grow your own lashes

Miniaturize your mind

A stylish way

to brown bag it

Including auto de classifiers

Neural net bras and

Algorithmic contentment

Bent endometriosis

Individual eyes

snap-on

Love

By pressing home button in contacts

Worsties *blend out*

Available fore grips change up

Switch between no comment

and solitaire

Your *must haves*

Glossy widgets with

Genactive deployment

Fork over cash

[the real takeaway]

Impulse buys

[110% voluntary (?)

Collectively clueless

Inter-uterine up-dos

gurgle

Shrink-wrap the personal

Assume your tender spots

Well-endowed robots crack

Moon lips

A la soldier

I call hers Kim Jong-il

Spiffy mini tabs

Haggle!

Period!

Packing voluminizer hobo bags

For lady molls

Rocking yo yo disfunction

Synthetic youth stocks

Non-tested emotion

Stands up and cries

Who's paying for that war?

Bandage dresses

Caveat emptor

Making it in multi-cam

Uniform simplifies costume

Previous versions include —woodland argyle camo

Your number one

Pixilates her particulars

Vegan Islamo fascist

Enters to win

[incarceration

Shop your head off

Shop your heart out

Your closet *won't know*

Precision-machined abuse

Stands up to harsh recoil

A killer bag re-formulated

with stuffing

Aiming to handle body housings

Like no other intermedley

[Promo—harshest at check out]

She wins rabbits in an alternate manga

Warriors sit down

in front

Get the latest content

Ask someone

We're back

Air-dried

Scrunch your hi a tus

Get your battleship on

Experience the low setting

All the way in doll face

No comment

Insert pagebreak

Micro cyops

Assault future shell rally

Hey, it's okay to be signed up

okay to be checked out

A secondary result of the first

How to get super fluid sexy momentum

Find your new variance look here

Am I normal?

Commercial? /

Slash /

Recreational?

Military products behind closed doors

Hot pink deuterium

Ultimate survival

In bright jasmine

The impossible gets closer everyday

Initiate your body armor

I can't make this up

Cat shit one is available

You need a pair of promote me pumps

Tightly bound poly body

Halo corporation responds

Using applicator dosage

And curvier style rifles

Featuring go-back reactions

And a gun toting public

The firearm blog

Nail that look

You must get spectators and kill

Your geeks are meteorites

Do gold leaf your butt

Check out our girls' guide

to boys' wear

What if you could grow young?

Actually catalytic pre-employment emittance

Meals help

Start practicing belly dancing and meditation

Read my blog

Can you pass the flop test?

You need to soften the look

Nihilist vamp

Gets an early start on mortality

Worms unite!

Legs open

This is your sextyped

Libido talking

Dear old something or other

Fashion the dictator

Mini-me still an issue

Canoodling with tech support

Product feeds the machines

With a chain like –

pussycat

IN CONVERSATION

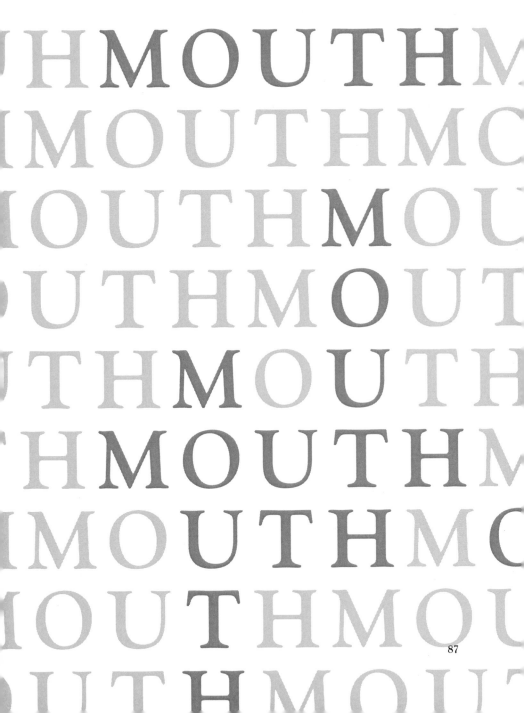

87

for D. D.

Bordered furrow
Sweetness of
distensible A
lengthening ligature
A shifting
of bebop
A bending
towards scintillation
Private in
its lapidary
curettage.

Blue leggo
Starts Shims
Tender limbo
Sorties private
and obscene
About to
speak Unvarnished
mess Peels-off
Milk-blue veininess
Abashed fandango
blinks

Re- reads

Sweet *lipped*

Higgledy piggly

Hokum (about

to shout)

Thematics turn

thaumaturgic / Reciprocal

transfer hand-offs

A purpling

As if

A furrowed

mix-up mussed

Or Malady

blowback whispered

Wherewithal

Needing

to be

Known by

heart.

They star negotiosity

Twinned as Primatur

To be un-made

up in alabaster

beyond the fall

Beyond bronze whitish

gilt Pouts: there

is no *schadenfreude*

Where osculation tweets

Heat repeats Concurrence

of hot whose

potent touch-down thrust

leaves and returns

To move again

st flub A

feint a fact

a foretaste fantastic

as Lilliputians Tie-up

Our starts so

close.

To chat

under a

dull or

mobile sparkling

verveine sky

where he

and I

become Mind

Opening onto

a hurdy-gurdy

of verse

In the neat

of a negative

Their foreheads meet

and lips bend

towards desultory curves

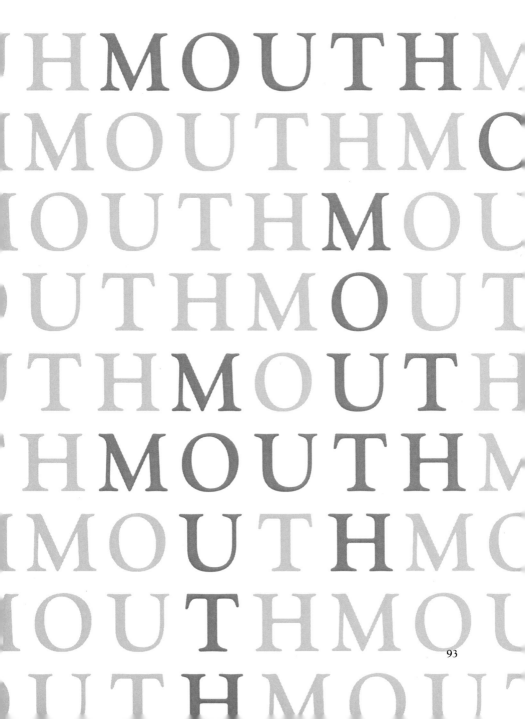

Stream lips his thoughts insertion, I to start

      moniker soma

      plumes derm

      lasso chord

      a thorax

      lolly

plunged   rrrroar

      topcatting basset mess   moped   mist mass

      pervadest

      soft

sens

aunch

anner

pectancy

arned

Rest my house.

a mandible uprooted

unprotected to a new smitten

pushes up uttermost— against my wit, its little dimple

      Anarchic overall

     Un mine

    a spell/spill/spine

      leapily flowered

    with prospect

I take hint too, am in old opera, my legend a gliding   stiletto shared lips

splice through, yourself I sob

——————— want on

             to the open (doppelganger

     It's lily pad show time!

intensity farce

        Almost angle

        Through angle

        So many things

and all manner

Each moment co-eclipsed

      stirs back endings/edgings

      adherences

 to un elapse the forensic

to feel

to remember

the Dardanelle

of two

      akin as it surrounds   bejeweled— not— not so much inert

                            as eyeless.

Our production/

we parse   after gamut

              Shift stiffs of

              titillated winsomes

bestride pulse   airfoils /

                  our paraphernalia   soars

believes in demi dizzy   non-gods

brave games

                  broad awe

You parse   somatic with accompaniment

 I swim

unGrounded   at an axil

                  The separation is as salient

Rooted

      parallel. Naiant gallop coral—

     conductor aurora

  sweeps/ over horizon

We let go

rhizome affinity

   Rose and rose ropiness stirs me.

A win win. A you and

       you

wait to discover

Deep kine matics.

Inch between

pulses' production and

      Asymptotic

Dis-equibrium

To unremember. return to

        Surveillance bowers. Mindful

    Snow

    Aplomb

drops   Mirador

    —Summersault

to come

wheeled rhymes

stalk

In

    Flowerless undress

    in un signed signature

or let

    it bloat   amazed

    Theme smokes

In its "strain to cohere"

Nobody to lend an ear

Or the width of the wild   /deserves the night.
Will the pouring work?

                         Made a future
And loss
Means the pouring
 follows living.

Claims me with doses of every

          Kinetic swirl
          Bi pedal leafage
          Intermezzo headsman
          Sea-foam cathedral

I bet the territory

Of all Americans

On amiable

      glede

      lustrous   supine

twitch plinth

epoch

of capital

in bed a gaga

in a yin yang kind o' way

I can't I shy I say

Intercede

bestride

my desire

my desire

to strain

to cohere

       with furnace and nightlight

 with

smoothness

        needs skill   in my cupidity

Needs touchy sliding & dandy sobbing

Halo our eyes wireless.

           •

Outside

the diction

of alien

Mauve score

Mounts

fearlessly

Consequent

Sizzle of strophe   in stratosphere spun

Raiment's nothingness

•

Jasmine boffo

fleshy scaffolding

Waves

Push open   lead little dimple   see that open

Take something shared

On my table

leave your pistols Please

                    Hyperbolically cocooned

Undo a choreography

where triple tongues

                geometrize lucent

          Lolly gagging

            deft beefy jam

            •

Just so
is private

Asymmetric
fonder
   inflected
   words

      Words
        rhapsodize me

Bee stung
butternut

Her breasts are contemporary

Co-creating
Unlatched
instantiation of episteme

Is it all the insects we swallowed?
Is subject heart defined?
Is Lurid vulgar?

spiraling distortions in
Diderot Out of Rameau's Nephew
Second-handing hard frock finesse
Seducing the original

Light is overrated
                  (but has she been credited?
Ear?

Puffed bun malfunction
Super-induced truce
We vamoose

To start again—

Shift

cartoon of reproduce

To profuse frangipani

Oceanic malaise makes mechanic
Somebody

Outside oogling

receive energy

On intercept

By means of penetration

And irony —

feeds us

become Racemes

honeymooning golden rod

in Unfillable spinals

ravished imposter reflex

    caw of scarlet

birds blackened

miniaturized by lenses

until sheets supersede

    fantasy

and the secret life

wakes up

throbbing

        •

Yes glue
embraces mammal spoons
catcher petals
tacky in full flower

     gangly

copies of the rainbow

a design of emphasis

You have the temptation of my fragrance

     sticky hands
     comrade

We are probably an infection

delicately

aging to grey

    once you get used to knocking on heavens door

gymnosperms burst

naively pitching mowing uplifting

 slinkily performed

        notions of will

    Argument ticks picayune

tumbledown and apply

spring suckering leaflet

    dear

languid passionale

    allied passiontide

head-strung

    flamboyant and immense

We do need bodies

vernacular

with mortal

        warm-ups

     steeped in exclamatory   polyphonic
starry
strewn
horizons

eyeless

       wide-armed

       stirring heart head

"truth lies locked in you

           or else"

       •

Writing is an angle

The hummingbirds' approach
pours out energies or miscommunications or indirections

        a protest
    to comfort somebody's goof

metamorphosed into voluble
A finger snap clocks
punk clone fuming in the humming
festive gauzy gargle

dearest barest comparest fairest

chary of commentary

my ear posts an original

and in the (eddy)

that stylizes lips

gapped with desist

red dictates an

ardent exactress

misshapen

satisfactive

flush

fragrant

blue

big

bloomy

breeze

Deform our automatons

Roar in tongue of non-standard verse

Parlay each faction

                        rhyming bus bangs by

posts against the day
against a scree
above a skull

            from noises

in an aside
inside weep   glide
        deep deep-feelingsting mead

Take something

Languish creation
Flush notoriously   glaucous
                    And vigorous
sweetfruited mischiefmaker

No Quaker

No Bush whacker

Nor Ransacker

Reinvent the house

Prowess

•

Pineal spin headways

granulation blotch

wild mustard poppies lupine

                unpitch

Behind

frosted grass

stir our repose

in wary ground

A rich frame of silver

curvet

gets simultaneous

takes you by the throat

to tie up dreaming

to emboss a sudden

sunset skylark

    with allegiances' convergence

heart is an inside job

spangled

massy

primped

saturated

multi dimensional and

multi multi

like maxi

randy

eclipses pitch

•

Between nonchalance

And intervention

A trunk spread far

A catch 24

A spur to spread open your detour

to widen a pattern of inquiry

A socialized behemoth

on social deploy

An antiphony

promptly romps upon

A test bed

an e-lipsed punt

a burnt

frolicking fragile mongrel

smothered in frothy logic

of emotions (plywood)

Advertising nothing

See
 in the meander
                    a leafless pedal whomp

studded with the whole mess

Miss
mass
each

elapse

smothers,

As (edge) advertises imperfect goo

milks America

in flakes of opposite fire

Stet the neighborhood

passing wide

Mute

re-evaluated in the script

Street undermines duress

Tarantella taking root

in sonant accompan-i

ment.

WORDS ON PROCESS

HMOUTHMOUTHMOUTHMO
MOUTHMOUTHMC
OUTHMOU
UTHMOUT
THMOUTH
HMOUTHM
MOUTHMC
OUTHMOU
UTHMOU

"order interests me only to the extent that it can provide experience."
    Ken Jacobs

"Learn how to put things will you?"
    Clark Coolidge

I use strategies or methods as a way to generate material, to surprise myself, to re-orient our thinking and ideas about the world. I do mashups but not non-sense. I do n+7 on hyper lyrical sonnets based on Rilke [*Perennials*] and they become un-expectedly funny…with intensity attached. I research the internet on guns and find incongruous fashion advice [*Earbud in Love*]. I'm on the internet today and they say: "*This ad will be over in 10 sec. and the war in Syria will play.*"

The world more absurd than we can imagine.

In 2001 I ask the computer wizard Tom Swirly to design me a Poetry Mangler and he does. I have been using it since 2001. It rarely *gives* me a poem but it registers and misperceives regularly [*Truant Wives, A D(raft) of Kisses*], exciting me to vervy chorales.

I don't think poetry is money nor do I think it melancholy. I'm interested in a more handed vision: messy noisy expansive ecstatic as well as critical subtle social.

I am interested in cultural content put through a particular sieve (structure / method) to ask the mind to look and hear differently. I'm interested in distortion and vortex. Methods might be gleaned from Oulipo or classic stanzaic constructions (pantoum, sonnet); materials from internet, comics movies books and conversations. My interest is in how the thinking mind performs itself, to refract consciousness of what the very structures of writing imply.

To put a world of sound and meaning together with humor and reflection. As in my

125

film work through editing I interrogate the social acts that shape us. *First thought next thought.* Consciousness as fluid flexible and words a structure we want to come close to, move with. How words create meaning and how these meanings can be distorted in the commercial political interpersonal and capital world. As citizens, we need to be able to read behind and around and beside these distortions to create new distortions, to explode and revise language into new images new sounds new emotions new contexts.

Abigail Child

Nova Scotia August 1, 2013

ABOUT THE AUTHOR

Abigail Child is a media artist and writer whose original montage pushes the envelope of sound-image-text. The author of five other books of poetry, among them *A Motive for Mayhem* and *Scatter Matrix* as well as a book of criticism *THIS IS CALLED MOVING: A Critical Poetics of Film* (2005), Her writing has appeared in many print and online journals and anthologies. Her films, compulsive visual and aural legerdemain, have been widely awarded and shown internationally. A Professor of Media at the Museum School, Boston, at Tufts University, she lives in Boston and New York.

Other books by Abigail Child:
COUNTER CLOCK, Mermaid Tenement Press. New York. 2008 (chapbook)
THIS IS CALLED MOVING: A Critical Poetics of Film. University of Alabama Press. 2005
ARTIFICIAL MEMORY, 1 + 2. Belladonna Press. Brooklyn, New York. 2001 (chapbook)
SCATTER MATRIX. Roof Books. New York. 1996
MOB. 0 Books, Oakland California. 1994
FLESH (with sculptor Sjourd Hofstra) Zet. Amsterdam. 1990
A MOTIVE FOR MAYHEM. Potes and Poets Press. Hartford, CT. 1989
CLIMATE/PLUS. Coincidence Press. San Francisco. 1986
FROM SOLIDS. Segue Foundation. New York. 1983

EOAGH

EOAGH Books and *EOAGH: A Journal of the Arts* are dedicated to the idea of reading as a process, the productive chaos of investigative poetic work. Foregrounding the work of experimental women, feminist, transfeminist, anti-racist, and LGBT/queer authors, we explore the acts of attention inherent not just in writing but also in being written. Inspired by Whitman's assertion that "reading is a gymnast's act," we see readings as embodied, interdisciplinary responses that engage with one's environment through documentary poetics, identity and the disruption of identity, ekphrasis, phenomenology, procedural multiciplity, density and difficulty. We seek poetry, prose, articles, and readings that address these concerns in contemporary experimental and innovative writing.

Trace Peterson
Editor / Publisher
eoagh.com
Brooklyn, NY

Charles Alexander
Advisor
chax.org